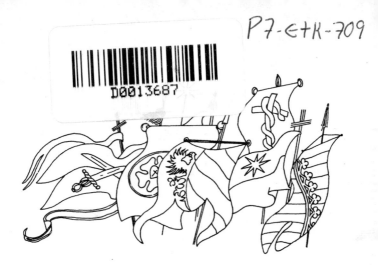

THE AUGSBURG CONFESSION

A Confession of Faith Presented in Augsburg
by certain Princes and Cities to His
Imperial Majesty Charles V
in the Year 1530

(Translated from the German text)

The Augsburg Confession
1980 Edition
from
The Book of Concord
Translated and Edited by
Theodore G. Tappert

© 1959 by Fortress Press

ISBN 0-8006-1385-6

Printed in the United States of America   *1-1385*

15   16   17

INTRODUCTION

Under date of Jan. 21, 1530, Emperor Charles V summoned an imperial diet to meet the following April in Augsburg Germany. He desired a united front in his military operations against the Turks, and this seemed to demand that an end be made of the religious disunity which had been introduced at home as a result of the Reformation. Accordingly he invited the princes and representatives of free cities in the empire to discuss the religious differences at the forthcoming diet in the hope of overcoming them and restoring unity. In keeping with this invitation the elector of Saxony asked his theologians in Wittenberg to prepare an account of the beliefs and

Bishops Square, Augsburg

practices in the churches of his land. Since a statement of doctrines, known as the Schwabach Articles, had already been prepared in the summer of 1529, all that seemed to be needed now was an additional statement concerning the changes in practice which had been made in the churches of Saxony. Such a statement was therefore prepared by the Wittenberg theologians, and since it was approved at a meeting in Torgau at the end of March, 1530, it is commonly referred to as the Torgau Articles.

Together with other documents, the Schwabach and the Torgau Articles were taken to Augsburg. There it was decided to make a common Lutheran statement, rather than merely a Saxon statement, of the account which was to be submitted to the emperor. Circumstances also demanded that it be made clear in the statement that Lutherans were not casually to be lumped together with all the other opponents of Rome, and other considerations suggested the desirability of emphasizing the agreements with Rome rather than the differences from Rome. All these factors played a part in determining the character of the document which was now prepared under the hands of Philip Melanchthon. The Schwabach Articles became the principal basis for the first part and the Torgau Articles became the principal basis for the second part of what came to be the Augsburg Confession. Luther, who was not present in Augsburg, was consulted through correspondence, but revisions and emendations were made to the very eve of the formal presentation to the emperor on June 25, 1530. Signed by seven princes and the representatives of two free cities, the confession immediately achieved peculiar importance as a public declaration of faith.

In accordance with the emperor's instructions, texts of the confession were prepared and presented in both German and Latin. The actual reading before the diet was from the German text, which may therefore be regarded as more official. Unfortunately neither the German nor the Latin text is extant in the exact forms in which these were submitted. However, more than fifty copies dating from the year 1530 have been found, including drafts which present various stages in the preparation before June 25 as well as copies with a variety of new changes in wording made after June 25. These versions have been the object of extended critical study on the part of many scholars, and a German and a Latin text have been reconstructed which can claim to be close to, even if not identical with, the documents presented to the emperor.

T.G.T.

PREFACE

Most serene, most mighty, invincible Emperor, most gracious Lord:

A short time ago Your Imperial Majesty graciously summoned a diet of the empire to convene here in Augsburg. In the summons Your Majesty indicated an earnest desire to deliberate concerning matters pertaining to the Turk, that traditional foe of ours and of the Christian religion, and how with continuing help he might effectively be resisted. The desire was also expressed for deliberation on what might be done about the dissension concerning our holy faith and the Christian religion, and to this end it was proposed to employ all diligence amicably and charitably to hear, understand, and weigh the judgments, opinions, and beliefs of the several parties among us, to unite the same in agreement on one Christian truth, to put aside whatever may not have been rightly interpreted or treated by either side,[1] to have all of us embrace and adhere to a single, true religion and live together in unity and in one fellowship and church, even as we are all enlisted under one Christ.[2] Inasmuch as we, the undersigned elector and princes and our associates, have been summoned for these purposes, together with other electors, princes, and estates,[3] we have complied with the command and can say without boasting that we were among the first to arrive.[4]

In connection with the matter pertaining to the faith and in conformity with the imperial summons, Your Imperial Majesty also graciously and earnestly requested[5] that each of the electors, princes, and estates should commit to writing and present, in German and Latin, his judgments, opinions, and beliefs with reference to the said errors, dissensions, and abuses. Accordingly, after due deliberation and counsel, it was decided last Wednesday that, in keeping with Your Majesty's wish, we should present our case in German and Latin today (Friday).[6] Wherefore, in dutiful obedience to Your Imperial Majesty, we offer and present a confession of our pastors' and preachers' teaching and of our own faith, setting forth how and in what manner, on the basis of the Holy Scriptures, these things are preached, taught, communicated, and embraced in our lands, principalities, dominions, cities, and territories.

If the other electors, princes, and estates also submit a similar written statement of their judgments and opinions, in Latin and German, we are prepared, in obedience to Your Imperial Majesty, our most gracious lord, to discuss with them and their associates, in so far as this can honorably be done, such practical and equitable ways as may restore unity. Thus the matters at issue between us may be presented in writing on both sides, they may be discussed amicably and charitably, our differences may be reconciled, and we may be united in one, true religion, even as we are all under one Christ and should confess and contend for Christ. All of this is in accord with Your Imperial Majesty's aforementioned summons. That it may be done according to divine truth we invoke almighty God in deepest humility and implore him to bestow his grace to this end. Amen.

If, however, our lords, friends, and associates who represent the electors, princes, and estates of the other party do not comply with the procedure intended by Your Imperial Majesty's summons, if no amicable and charitable negotiations take place between us, and if no results are attained, nevertheless we on our part shall not omit doing anything, in so far as God and conscience allow, that may serve the cause of Christian unity. Of this Your Imperial Majesty, our aforementioned friends (the electors, princes, and estates), and every lover of the Christian religion who is concerned about these questions will be graciously and sufficiently assured from what follows in the confession which we and our associates submit.

we offer and present a confession...

In the past[7] Your Imperial Majesty graciously gave assurance to the electors, princes, and estates of the empire, especially in a public instruction at the diet in Spires in 1526, that for reasons there stated Your Imperial Majesty was not disposed to render decisions in matters pertaining to our holy faith but would diligently urge it upon the pope to call a council. Again, by means of a written instruction at the last diet in Spires a year ago, the electors, princes, and estates of the empire were, among other things, informed and notified by Your Imperial Majesty's viceroy (His Royal Majesty of Hungary and Bohemia, etc.) and by Your Imperial Majesty's orator and appointed commissioners, that Your Imperial Majesty's viceroy, administrators, and councilors of the imperial government (together with the absent electors, princes, and representatives of the estates) who were assembled at the diet convened in Ratisbon[8] had considered the proposal concerning a general council and acknowledged that it would be profitable to have such a council called. Since the relations between Your Imperial Majesty and the pope were improving and were progressing toward a good, Christian understanding,[9] Your Imperial Majesty was sure that the pope would not refuse to call a general council, and so Your Imperial Majesty graciously offered to promote and bring about the calling of such a general council by the pope, along with Your Imperial Majesty, at the earliest opportunity and to allow no hindrance to be put in the way.

If the outcome should be such as we mentioned above,[10] we offer in full obedience, even beyond what is required, to participate in such a general, free, and Christian council as the electors, princes, and estates have with the highest and best motives requested in all the diets of the empire which have been held during Your Imperial Majesty's reign. We have at various times made our protestations and appeals concerning these most weighty matters, and have done so in legal form and procedure. To these we declare our continuing adherence, and we shall not be turned aside from our position by these or any following negotiations (unless the matters in dissension are finally heard, amicably weighed, charitably settled, and brought to Christian concord in accordance with Your Imperial Majesty's summons) as we herewith publicly witness and assert. This is our confession and that of our associates, and it is specifically stated, article by article, in what follows.

ARTICLES OF FAITH AND DOCTRINE

I. [GOD][1]

We unanimously hold and teach, in accordance with the decree of the Council of Nicaea,[2] that there is one divine essence, which is called and which is truly God, and that there are three persons in this one divine essence, equal in power and alike eternal: God the Father, God the Son, God the Holy Spirit. All three are one divine essence, eternal, without division, without end, of infinite power, wisdom, and goodness, one creator and preserver of all things visible and invisible. The word "person" is to be understood as the Fathers employed the term in this connection, not as a part or a property of another but as that which exists of itself.[3]

Therefore all the heresies which are contrary to this article are rejected. Among these are the heresy of the Manichaeans,[4] who assert that there are two gods, one good and one evil; also that of the Valentinians,[5] Arians,[6] Eunomians,[7] Mohammedans,[8] and others like them; also that of the Samosatenes,[9] old and new, who hold that there

All the heresies which are contrary to this article are rejected.

is only one person and sophistically assert that the other two, the Word and the Holy Spirit, are not necessarily distinct persons but that the Word signifies a physical word or voice and that the Holy Spirit is a movement induced in creatures.

II. [ORIGINAL SIN]

It is also taught among us that since the fall of Adam all men who are born according to the course of nature are conceived and born in sin. That is, all men are full of evil lust and inclinations from their mothers' wombs and are unable by nature to have true fear of God and true faith in God. Moreover, this inborn sickness and hereditary sin[1] is truly sin and condemns to the eternal wrath of God all those who are not born again through Baptism and the Holy Spirit.

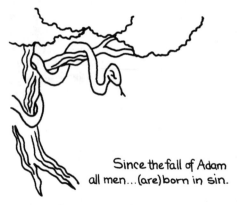

Since the fall of Adam
all men...(are) born in sin.

Rejected in this connection are the Pelagians[2] and others who deny that original sin is sin, for they hold that natural man is made righteous by his own powers, thus disparaging the sufferings and merit of Christ.

III. [THE SON OF GOD]

It is also taught among us that God the Son became man, born of the virgin Mary, and that the two natures, divine and human, are so inseparably united in one person that there is one Christ, true God and true man, who was truly born, suffered, was crucified, died, and was buried in order to be a sacrifice not only for original sin but also for all other sins and to propitiate God's wrath. The same Christ also descended into hell, truly rose from the dead on the third day, ascended into heaven, and sits on the right hand of God, that he may eternally rule and have dominion over all creatures, that through the Holy Spirit he may sanctify, purify, strengthen, and comfort all who believe in him, that he may bestow on them life and every grace and blessing, and that he may protect and defend them against the devil and against sin. The same Lord Christ will return openly to judge the living and the dead, as stated in the Apostles' Creed.

IV. [JUSTIFICATION]

It is also taught among us that we cannot obtain forgiveness of sin and righteousness before God by our own merits, works, or satisfactions, but that we receive forgiveness of sin and become righteous before God by grace, for Christ's sake, through faith, when we believe that Christ suffered for us and that for his sake our sin is forgiven and righteousness and eternal life are given to us. For God will regard and reckon this faith as righteousness, as Paul says in Romans 3:21–26 and 4:5.

V. [THE OFFICE OF THE MINISTRY][1]

To obtain such faith God instituted the office of the ministry, that is, provided the Gospel and the sacraments.

Through these, as through means, he gives the Holy Spirit, who works faith, when and where he pleases, in those who hear the Gospel. And the Gospel teaches that we have a gracious God, not by our own merits but by the merit of Christ, when we believe this.

Condemned are the Anabaptists and others[2] who teach that the Holy Spirit comes to us through our own preparations, thoughts, and works without the external word of the Gospel.

VI. [THE NEW OBEDIENCE]

It is also taught among us that such faith should produce good fruits and good works and that we must do all such good works as God has commanded,[1] but we should do them for God's sake and not place our trust in them as if thereby to merit favor before God. For we receive forgiveness of sin and righteousness through faith in Christ, as Christ himself says, "So you also, when you have done all that is commanded you, say, 'We are unworthy servants' " (Luke 17:10). The Fathers also teach thus, for Ambrose says, "It is ordained of God that whoever believes in Christ shall be saved, and he shall have forgiveness of sins, not through works but through faith alone, without merit."[2]

VII. [THE CHURCH]

It is also taught among us that one holy Christian church will be and remain forever. This is the assembly of all believers among whom the Gospel is preached in its purity and the holy sacraments are administered according to the Gospel. For it is sufficient for the true unity of the Christian church that the Gospel be preached in conformity with a pure understanding of it and that the sacraments be administered in accordance with the divine Word. It is not necessary for the true unity of the Christian church that ceremonies, instituted by men, should be observed uni-

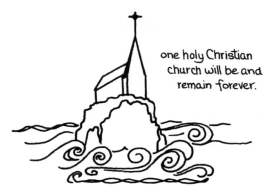

one holy Christian church will be and remain forever.

formly in all places. It is as Paul says in Eph. 4:4, 5, "There is one body and one Spirit, just as you were called to the one hope that belongs to your call, one Lord, one faith, one baptism."

VIII. [What the Church Is]

Again, although the Christian church, properly speaking, is nothing else than the assembly of all believers and saints, yet because in this life many false Christians, hypocrites, and even open sinners remain among the godly, the sacraments are efficacious even if the priests who administer them are wicked men, for as Christ himself indicated, "The Pharisees sit on Moses' seat" (Matt. 23:2).

Accordingly the Donatists[1] and all others who hold contrary views are condemned.

IX. Baptism

It is taught among us that Baptism is necessary and that grace is offered through it. Children, too, should be baptized, for in Baptism they are committed to God and become acceptable to him.

On this account the Anabaptists who teach that infant Baptism is not right are rejected.

X. The Holy Supper of our Lord

It is taught among us that the true body and blood of Christ are really present in the Supper of our Lord under the form of bread and wine and are there distributed and received. The contrary doctrine is therefore rejected.

XI. Confession

It is taught among us that private absolution should be retained and not allowed to fall into disuse. However, in confession it is not necessary to enumerate all trespasses and sins,[1] for this is impossible. Ps. 19:12, "Who can discern his errors?"

XII. Repentance

It is taught among us that those who sin after Baptism receive forgiveness of sin whenever they come to repentance, and absolution should not be denied them by the church. Properly speaking, true repentance is nothing else than to have contrition and sorrow, or terror, on account of sin, and yet at the same time to believe the Gospel and absolution (namely, that sin has been forgiven and grace has been obtained through Christ), and this faith will comfort the heart and again set it at rest.[1] Amendment of life and the forsaking of sin should then follow, for these must be the fruits of repentance, as John says, "Bear fruit that befits repentance" (Matt. 3:8).

Rejected here are those who teach that persons who have once become godly cannot fall again.[2]

Condemned on the other hand are the Novatians[3] who denied absolution to such as had sinned after Baptism.

Rejected also are those who teach that forgiveness of sin is not obtained through faith but through the satisfactions made by man.

XIII. The Use of the Sacraments

It is taught among us that the sacraments were instituted not only to be signs by which people might be identified outwardly as Christians, but that they are signs and testimonies of God's will toward us for the purpose of awakening and strengthening our faith. For this reason they require faith, and they are rightly used when they are received in faith and for the purpose of strengthening faith.

XIV. Order in the Church

It is taught among us that nobody should publicly teach or preach or administer the sacraments in the church without a regular call.

XV. Church Usages

With regard to church usages that have been established by men, it is taught among us that those usages are to be observed which may be observed without sin and which contribute to peace and good order in the church, among them being certain holy days, festivals,[1] and the like. Yet we accompany these observances with instruction so that consciences may not be burdened by the notion that such things are necessary for salvation. Moreover it is taught that all ordinances and traditions instituted by men for the purpose of propitiating God and earning grace are contrary to the Gospel and the teaching about faith in Christ. Accordingly monastic vows and other traditions concerning distinctions of foods, days, etc.,[2] by which it is intended to earn grace and make satisfaction for sin, are useless and contrary to the Gospel.

XVI. Civil Government

It is taught among us that all government in the world and all established rule and laws were instituted and ordained by God for the sake of good order, and that Christians may without sin occupy civil offices or serve as princes and judges, render decisions and pass sentence according to imperial and other existing laws, punish evildoers with the sword, engage in just wars, serve as soldiers, buy and sell, take required oaths, possess property, be married, etc.

Condemned here are the Anabaptists who teach that none of the things indicated above is Christian.[1]

Also condemned are those who teach that Christian perfection requires the forsaking of house and home, wife and child, and the renunciation of such activities as are mentioned above.[2] Actually, true perfection consists alone of proper fear of God and real faith in God, for the Gospel does not teach an outward and temporal but an inward and eternal mode of existence and righteousness of the heart. The Gospel does not overthrow civil authority, the state, and marriage but requires that all these be kept as true orders of God[3] and that everyone, each according to his own calling, manifest Christian love and genuine good works in his station of life. Accordingly Christians are obliged to be subject to civil authority and obey its commands and laws in all that can be done without sin. But when commands of the civil authority cannot be obeyed without sin, we must obey God rather than men (Acts 5:29).

..each according to his own calling, manifest Christian love.

XVII. [The Return of Christ to Judgment]

It is also taught among us that our Lord Jesus Christ will return on the last day for judgment and will raise up all the dead, to give eternal life and everlasting joy to believers and the elect but to condemn ungodly men and the devil to hell and eternal punishment.

Rejected, therefore, are the Anabaptists who teach that the devil and condemned men will not suffer eternal pain and torment.[1]

Rejected, too, are certain Jewish opinions which are even now making an appearance and which teach that, before the resurrection of the dead, saints and godly men will possess a worldly kingdom and annihilate all the godless.[2]

XVIII. Freedom of the Will

It is also taught among us that man possesses some measure of freedom of the will which enables him to live an outwardly honorable life and to make choices among the things that reason comprehends. But without the grace, help, and activity of the Holy Spirit man is not capable of making himself acceptable to God, of fearing God and believing in God with his whole heart, or of expelling inborn evil lusts from his heart. This is accomplished by the Holy Spirit, who is given through the Word of God, for Paul says in I Cor. 2:14, "Natural man does not receive the gifts of the Spirit of God."

freedom
to choose
good
or evil

In order that it may be evident that this teaching is no novelty, the clear words of Augustine on free will are here quoted from the third book of his *Hypognosticon*:[1] "We concede that all men have a free will, for all have a natural, innate understanding and reason. However, this does not enable them to act in matters pertaining to God (such as loving God with their whole heart or fearing him), for it is only in the outward acts of this life that they have freedom to choose good or evil. By good I mean what they are capable of by nature: whether or not to labor in the fields, whether or not to eat or drink or visit a friend, whether to dress or undress, whether to build a house, take a wife, engage in a trade, or do whatever else may be good and profitable. None of these is or exists without God, but all things are from him and through him. On the other hand, by his own choice man can also undertake evil, as when he wills to kneel before an idol, commit murder, etc."[2]

XIX. The Cause of Sin

It is taught among us that although almighty God has created and still preserves nature, yet sin is caused in all wicked men and despisers of God by the perverted will. This is the will of the devil and of all ungodly men; as soon as God withdraws his support, the will turns away from God to evil. It is as Christ says in John 8:44, "When the devil lies, he speaks according to his own nature."

XX. Faith and Good Works

Our teachers have been falsely accused of forbidding good works. Their writings on the Ten Commandments, and other writings as well, show that they have given good and profitable accounts and instructions concerning true Christian estates and works. About these little was taught in former times, when for the most part sermons were concerned with childish and useless works like rosaries, the cult of saints, monasticism, pilgrimages, appointed fasts, holy days, brotherhoods,[1] etc. Our opponents no longer praise these useless works so highly as they once did, and they have also learned to speak now of faith, about which they did not preach at all in former times. They do not teach now that we become righteous before God by our works alone, but they add faith in Christ and say that faith and works make us righteous before God. This teaching may offer a little more comfort than the teaching that we are to rely solely on our works.

Since the teaching about faith, which is the chief article in the Christian life, has been neglected so long (as all must admit) while nothing but works was preached everywhere, our people have been instructed as follows:

We begin by teaching that our works cannot reconcile us with God or obtain grace for us, for this happens only through faith, that is, when we believe that our sins are forgiven for Christ's sake, who alone is the mediator who reconciles the Father. Whoever imagines that he can accomplish this by works, or that he can merit grace, despises Christ and seeks his own way to God, contrary to the Gospel.

This teaching about faith is plainly and clearly treated by Paul in many passages, especially in Eph. 2:8, 9, "For by grace you have been saved through faith; and this is not your own doing, it is the gift of God—not because of works, lest any man should boast," etc.

That no new interpretation is here introduced can be demonstrated from Augustine, who discusses this question thoroughly and teaches the same thing, namely, that we obtain grace and are justified before God through faith in Christ and not through works. His whole book, *De spiritu et litera,* [2] proves this.

Although this teaching is held in great contempt among untried people, yet it is a matter of experience that weak and terrified consciences find it most comforting and salutary. The conscience cannot come to rest and peace through works, but only through faith, that is, when it is assured and knows that for Christ's sake it has a gracious God, as Paul says in Rom. 5:1, "Since we are justified by faith, we have peace with God."

In former times this comfort was not heard in preaching, but poor consciences were driven to rely on their own efforts, and all sorts of works were undertaken. Some were driven by their conscience into monasteries in the hope that there they might merit grace through monastic life. Others devised other works for the purpose of earning grace and making satisfaction for sins. Many of them discovered that they did not obtain peace by such means. It was therefore necessary to preach this doctrine about faith in Christ and diligently to apply it in order that men may know that the grace of God is appropriated without merits, through faith alone.

Instruction is also given among us to show that the faith here spoken of is not that possessed by the devil and the ungodly,[3] who also believe the history of Christ's suffering and his resurrection from the dead, but we mean such true faith as believes that we receive grace and forgiveness of sin through Christ.

Whoever knows that in Christ he has a gracious God, truly knows God, calls upon him, and is not, like the heathen, without God. For the devil and the ungodly do not believe this article concerning the forgiveness of sin, and so they are at enmity with God, cannot call upon him, and have no hope of receiving good from him. Therefore, as has just been indicated, the Scriptures speak of faith but do not mean by it such knowledge as the devil and ungodly men possess. Heb. 11:1 teaches about faith in such a way as to make it clear that faith is not merely a knowledge of historical events but is a confidence

. . . the heart is moved to do good works.

in God and in the fulfillment of his promises. Augustine[4] also reminds us that we should understand the word "faith" in the Scriptures to mean confidence in God, assurance that God is gracious to us, and not merely such a knowledge of historical events as the devil also possesses.

It is also taught among us that good works should and must be done, not that we are to rely on them to earn grace but that we may do God's will and glorify him. It is always faith alone that apprehends grace and forgiveness of sin. When through faith the Holy Spirit is given, the heart is moved to do good works. Before that, when it is without the Holy Spirit, the heart is too weak. Moreover, it is in the power of the devil, who drives poor human beings into many sins. We see this in the philosophers who undertook to lead honorable and blameless lives; they failed to accomplish this, and instead fell into many great and open sins. This is what happens when a man is without true faith and the Holy Spirit and governs himself by his own human strength alone.

Consequently this teaching concerning faith is not to be accused of forbidding good works but is rather to be praised for teaching that good works are to be done and for offering help as to how they may be done. For without faith and without Christ human nature and human strength are much too weak to do good works, call upon God, have patience in suffering, love one's neighbor, diligently engage in callings which are commanded, render obedience, avoid evil lusts, etc. Such great and genuine works cannot be done without the help of Christ, as he himself says in John 15:5, "Apart from me you can do nothing."

XXI. The Cult of Saints

It is also taught among us that saints should be kept in remembrance so that our faith may be strengthened when

their good works
are to be an
example for us

we see what grace they received and how they were sustained by faith. Moreover, their good works are to be an example for us, each of us in his own calling. So His Imperial Majesty may in salutary and godly fashion imitate the example of David in making war on the Turk, for both are incumbents of a royal office which demands the defense and protection of their subjects.

However, it cannot be proved from the Scriptures that we are to invoke saints or seek help from them. "For there is one mediator between God and men, Christ Jesus" (I Tim. 2:5), who is the only saviour, the only highpriest, advocate, and intercessor before God (Rom. 8:34). He alone has promised to hear our prayers. Moreover, according to the Scriptures, the highest form of divine service is sincerely to seek and call upon this same Jesus Christ in every time of need. "If anyone sins, we have an advocate with the Father, Jesus Christ the righteous" (I John 2:1).

This is just about a summary of the doctrines that are preached and taught in our churches for proper Christian instruction, the consolation of consciences, and the amendment of believers. Certainly we should not wish to put our own souls and consciences in grave peril before God by misusing his name or Word, nor should we wish to bequeath to our children and posterity any other teaching than that which agrees with the pure Word of God and Christian truth. Since this teaching is grounded clearly on the Holy Scriptures and is not contrary or opposed to that of the universal Christian church, or even of the Roman church (in so far as the latter's teaching is reflected in the writings of the Fathers),[1] we think that our opponents cannot disagree with us in the articles set forth above. Therefore, those who presume to reject, avoid, and separate from our churches as if our teaching were heretical, act in an unkind and hasty fashion, contrary to all Christian unity and love, and do so without any solid basis of divine command or Scripture. The dispute and dissension are concerned chiefly with various traditions and abuses. Since, then, there is nothing unfounded or defective in the principal articles and since this our confession is seen to be godly and Christian, the bishops should in all fairness act more leniently, even if there were some defect among us in regard to traditions, although we hope to offer firm grounds and reasons why we have changed certain traditions and abuses.

this teaching is
grounded clearly
on Holy Scripture

ARTICLES ABOUT MATTERS IN DISPUTE, IN WHICH AN ACCOUNT IS GIVEN OF THE ABUSES WHICH HAVE BEEN CORRECTED

From the above it is manifest that nothing is taught in our churches concerning articles of faith that is contrary to the Holy Scriptures or what is common to the Christian church. However, inasmuch as some abuses have been corrected (some of the abuses having crept in over the years and others of them having been introduced with violence), we are obliged by our circumstances to give an account of them and to indicate our reasons for permitting changes in these cases in order that Your Imperial Majesty may perceive that we have not acted in an unchristian and frivolous manner but have been compelled by God's command (which is rightly to be regarded as above all custom) to allow such changes.

XXII. Both Kinds in the Sacrament

Among us both kinds are given to laymen in the sacrament. The reason is that there is a clear command and order of Christ, "Drink of it, all of you" (Matt. 26:27). Concerning the chalice Christ here commands with clear words that all should drink of it.

In order that no one might question these words and interpret them as if they apply only to priests, Paul shows in I Cor. 11:20ff. that the whole assembly of the congregation in Corinth received both kinds. This usage continued in the church for a long time, as can be demonstrated from history and from writings of the Fathers.[1] In several places Cyprian mentions that the cup was given to laymen in his time.[2] St. Jerome also states that the priests who administered the sacrament distributed the blood of Christ to the people.[3] Pope Gelasius himself ordered that the sacrament was not to be divided.[4] Not a single canon can be found which requires the reception of only one kind. Nobody knows when or through whom this custom of receiving only one kind was introduced, although Cardinal Cusanus mentions when the use was approved.[5] It is evident that such a custom, introduced contrary to God's command and also contrary to the ancient canons, is unjust. Accordingly it is not proper to burden the consciences of those who desire to observe the sacrament according to Christ's institution or to compel them to act contrary to the arrangement of our Lord Christ. Because the division of the sacrament is contrary to the institution of Christ, the customary carrying about of the sacrament in processions is also omitted by us.[6]

XXIII. The Marriage of Priests

Among all people, both of high and low degree, there has been loud complaint throughout the world concerning the flagrant immorality and the dissolute life of priests who were not able to remain continent and who went so far as to engage in abominable vices. In order to avoid such unbecoming offense, adultery, and other lechery, some of our priests have entered the married state. They have given as their reason that they have been impelled and moved to take this step by the great distress of their consciences, especially since the Scriptures clearly assert that the estate of marriage was instituted by the Lord God to avoid immorality, for Paul says, "Because of the temptation to immorality, each man should have his own wife" (I Cor. 7:3), and again, "It is better to marry than to be aflame with passion" (I Cor. 7:9). Moreover, when Christ said in Matt. 19:11, "Not all men can receive this precept,'' he indicated that few people have the gift of living in celibacy, and he certainly knew man's nature. God created man as male and female according to Gen. 1:27. Experience has made it all too manifest whether or not it lies in human power and ability to improve or change the creation of God the supreme Majesty, by means of human resolutions or vows without a special gift or grace of God. What good has resulted? What honest and chaste manner of life, what Christian, upright, and honorable sort of conduct has resulted in many cases? It is well known what terrible torment and frightful disturbance of conscience many have experienced on their deathbeds on this account, and many have themselves acknowledged this. Since God's Word and command cannot be altered by any human vows or laws, our priests and other clergy have taken wives to themselves for these and other reasons and causes.

It can be demonstrated from history and from the writings of the Fathers that it was customary for priests and deacons to marry in the Christian church of former times. Paul therefore said in I Tim. 3:2, "A bishop must be above reproach, married only once." It was only four hundred years ago that the priests in Germany were com-

god...instituted marriage...

pelled by force to take the vows of celibacy.[1] At that time there was such serious and strong resistance that an archbishop of Mayence[2] who had published the new papal decree was almost killed during an uprising of the entire body of priests. The decree concerning celibacy was at once enforced so hastily and indecently that the pope at that time not only forbade future marriages of priests but also broke up the marriages which were of long standing. This was of course not only contrary to all divine, natural, and civil law, but was also utterly opposed and contrary to the canons which the popes had themselves made and to the decisions of the most renowned councils.[3]

Many devout and intelligent people in high station have expressed similar opinions and the misgivings that such enforced celibacy and such prohibition of marriage (which God himself instituted and left free to man) never produced any good but rather gave occasion for many great and evil vices and much scandal. As his biography shows, even one of the popes, Pius II, often said and allowed himself to be quoted as saying that while there may well have been some reasons for prohibiting the marriage of clergymen, there were now more important, better, and weightier reasons for permitting them to be married.[4] There is no doubt that Pope Pius, as a prudent and intelligent man, made this statement because of grave misgivings.

In loyalty to Your Imperial Majesty we therefore feel confident that, as a most renowned Christian emperor, Your Majesty will graciously take into account the fact that, in these last times of which the Scriptures prophesy, the world is growing worse and men are becoming weaker and more infirm.

Therefore it is most necessary, profitable, and Christian to recognize this fact in order that the prohibition of marriage may not cause worse and more disgraceful lewdness and vice to prevail in German lands. No one is able to alter or arrange such matters in a better or wiser way than God himself, who instituted marriage to aid human infirmity and prevent unchastity.

The old canons also state that it is sometimes necessary to relax severity and rigor for the sake of human weakness and to prevent and avoid greater offense.[5]

In this case relaxation would certainly be both Christian and very necessary. How would the marriage of priests and the clergy, and especially of the pastors and others who are to minister to the church, be of disadvantage to the Christian church as a whole? If this hard prohibition of marriage is to continue longer, there may be a shortage of priests and pastors in the future.

As we have observed, the assertion that priests and clergymen may marry is based on God's Word and command. Besides, history demonstrates both that priests were married and that the vow of celibacy has been the cause of so much frightful and unchristian offense, so much adultery, and such terrible, shocking immorality and abominable vice that even some honest men among the cathedral clergy and some of the courtiers in Rome have often acknowledged this and have complained that such vices among the clergy would, on account of their abomination and prevalence, arouse the wrath of God. It is therefore deplorable that Christian marriage has not only been forbidden but has in many places been swiftly punished, as if it were a great crime, in spite of the fact that in the Holy Scriptures God commanded that marriage be held in honor. Marriage has also been highly praised in the imperial laws and in all states in which there have been laws and justice. Only in our time does one begin to persecute innocent people simply because they are married—and especially priests, who above all others should be spared—although this is done contrary not only to divine law but also to canon law. In I Tim. 4:1, 3 the apostle

Paul calls the teaching that forbids marriage a doctrine of the devil. Christ himself asserts that the devil is a murderer from the beginning (John 8:44). These two statements fit together well, for it must be a doctrine of the devil to forbid marriage and then to be so bold as to maintain such a teaching with the shedding of blood.

However, just as no human law can alter or abolish a command of God, neither can any vow alter a command of God. St. Cyprian therefore offered the counsel that women who were unable to keep their vows of chastity should marry. He wrote in his eleventh letter, "If they are unwilling or unable to keep their chastity, it is better for them to marry than to fall into the fire through their lusts, and they should see to it that they do not give their brothers and sisters occasion for offense."[6]

In addition, all the canons show great leniency and fairness toward those who have made vows in their youth[7] —and most of the priests and monks entered into their estates ignorantly when they were young.

XXIV. The Mass

We are unjustly accused of having abolished the Mass.[1] Without boasting, it is manifest that the Mass is observed among us with greater devotion and more earnestness than among our opponents. Moreover, the people are instructed often and with great diligence concerning the holy sacrament, why it was instituted, and how it is to be used (namely, as a comfort for terrified consciences) in order that the people may be drawn to the Communion and Mass. The people are also given instruction about other false teachings concerning the sacrament. Meanwhile no conspicuous changes have been made in the public ceremonies of the Mass, except that in certain places German hymns are sung in addition to the Latin responses for the instruction and exercise of the people. After all, the chief purpose of all ceremonies is to teach the people what they need to know about Christ.

Before our time, however, the Mass came to be misused in many ways, as is well known, by turning it into a sort of fair, by buying and selling it, and by observing it in almost all churches for a monetary consideration. Such abuses were often condemned by learned and devout men even before our time.[2] Then when our preachers preached about these things and the priests were reminded of the terrible responsibility which should properly concern every Christian (namely, that whoever uses the sacrament unworthily is guilty of the body and blood of Christ),[3] such mercenary Masses and private Masses,[4] which had hitherto been held under compulsion for the sake of revenues and stipends, were discontinued in our churches.

no sacrifice...
except the one
death of Christ.

At the same time the abominable error was condemned according to which it was taught that our Lord Christ had by his death made satisfaction only for original sin, and had instituted the Mass as a sacrifice for other sins. This transformed the Mass into a sacrifice for the living and the dead, a sacrifice by means of which sin was taken away and God was reconciled. Thereupon followed a debate as to whether one Mass held for many people merited as much as a special Mass held for an individual. Out of this grew the countless multiplication of Masses, by the performance of which men expected to get everything they needed from God. Meanwhile faith in Christ and true service of God were forgotten.

Demanded without doubt by the necessity of such circumstances, instruction was given so that our people might know how the sacrament is to be used rightly. They were taught, first of all, that the Scriptures show in many places that there is no sacrifice for original sin, or for any other sin, except the one death of Christ. For it is written in the Epistle to the Hebrews that Christ offered himself once and by this offering made satisfaction for all sin.[5] It is an unprecedented novelty in church doctrine that Christ's death should have made satisfaction only for original sin and not for other sins as well. Accordingly it is to be hoped that everyone will understand that this error is not unjustly condemned.

In the second place, St. Paul taught that we obtain grace before God through faith and not through works. Manifestly contrary to this teaching is the misuse of the Mass by those who think that grace is obtained through the performance of this work, for it is well known that the Mass is used to remove sin and obtain grace and all sorts of benefits from God, not only for the priest himself but also for the whole world and for others, both living and dead.

In the third place, the holy sacrament was not instituted to make provision for a sacrifice for sin—for the sacrifice has already taken place—but to awaken our faith and comfort our consciences when we perceive that through the sacrament grace and forgiveness of sin are promised us by Christ. Accordingly the sacrament requires faith, and without faith it is used in vain.

Inasmuch, then, as the Mass is not a sacrifice to remove the sins of others, whether living or dead, but should be a Communion in which the priest and others receive the sacrament for themselves, it is observed among us in the following manner: On holy days, and at other times when communicants are present, Mass is held and those who desire it are communicated. Thus the Mass is preserved among us in its proper use, the use which was formerly observed in the church and which can be proved by St. Paul's statement in I Cor. 11:20ff. and by many statements of the Fathers. For Chrysostom reports how the priest stood every day, inviting some to Communion and forbidding others to approach.[6] The ancient canons also indicate that one man officiated and communicated the other priests and deacons, for the words of the Nicene canon read, "After the priests the deacons shall receive the sacrament in order from the bishop or priest."[7]

Since, therefore, no novelty has been introduced which did not exist in the church from ancient times, and since no conspicuous change has been made in the public ceremonies of the Mass except that other unnecessary Masses which were held in addition to the parochial Mass, probably through abuse, have been discontinued, this manner of holding Mass ought not in fairness be condemned as heretical or unchristian. In times past, even in large churches where there were many people, Mass was not held on every day that the people assembled, for according to the Tripartite History, Book 9, on Wednesday and Friday the Scriptures were read and expounded in Alexandria, and otherwise these services were held without Mass.[8]

XXV. Confession

Confession has not been abolished by the preachers on

our side. The custom has been retained among us of not administering the sacrament to those who have not previously been examined and absolved. At the same time the people are carefully instructed concerning the consolation of the Word of absolution so that they may esteem absolution as a great and precious thing. It is not the voice or word of the man who speaks it, but it is the Word of God, who forgives sin, for it is spoken in God's stead and by God's command. We teach with great diligence about this command and power of keys and how comforting and necessary it is for terrified consciences. We also teach that God requires us to believe this absolution as much as if we heard God's voice from heaven, that we should joyfully comfort ourselves with absolution, and that we should know that through such faith we obtain forgiveness of sins. In former times the preachers who taught much about confession never mentioned a word concerning these necessary matters but only tormented consciences with long enumerations of sins, with satisfactions, with indulgences, with pilgrimages and the like. Many of our opponents themselves acknowledge that we have written about and treated of true Christian repentance in a more fitting fashion than had been done for a long time.

not necessary to enumerate all trespasses...

Concerning confession we teach that no one should be compelled to recount sins in detail, for this is impossible. As the psalmist says, "Who can discern his errors?"[1] Jeremiah also says, "The heart is desperately corrupt; who can understand it?"[2] Our wretched human nature is so deeply submerged in sins that it is unable to perceive or know them all, and if we were to be absolved only from those which we can enumerate we would be helped but little. On this account there is no need to compel people to give a detailed account of their sins. That this was also the view of the Fathers can be seen in Dist. I, *De poenitentia,* where these words of Chrysostom are quoted: "I do not say that you should expose yourself in public or should accuse yourself before others, but obey the prophet who says, 'Show your way to the Lord.'[3] Therefore confess to the Lord God, the true judge, in your prayer, telling him of your sins not with your tongue but in your conscience."[4] Here it can be clearly seen that Chrysostom does not require a detailed enumeration of sins. The marginal note in *De poenitentia,* Dist. 5,[5] also teaches that such confession is not commanded by the Scriptures but was instituted by the church. Yet the preachers on our side diligently teach that confession is to be retained for the sake of absolution (which is its chief and most important part), for the consolation of terrified consciences, and also for other reasons.

XXVI. The Distinction of Foods

In former times men taught, preached, and wrote that distinctions among foods and similar traditions which had been instituted by men serve to earn grace and make satisfaction for sin.[1] For this reason new fasts, new ceremonies, new orders, and the like were invented daily, and were ardently and urgently promoted, as if these were a necessary service of God by means of which grace would be earned if they were observed and a great sin committed if they were omitted. Many harmful errors in the church have resulted from this.

In the first place, the grace of Christ and the teaching concerning faith are thereby obscured, and yet the Gospel earnestly urges them upon us and strongly insists that we regard the merit of Christ as something great and precious and know that faith in Christ is to be esteemed far above all works. On this account St. Paul contended mightily against the law of Moses and against human tradition so that we should learn that we do not become good in God's sight by our works but that it is only through faith in Christ that we obtain grace for Christ's sake. This teaching has been almost completely extinguished by those who have taught that grace is to be earned by prescribed fasts, distinctions among foods, vestments, etc.

In the second place, such traditions have also obscured the commands of God, for these traditions were exalted far above God's commands. This also was regarded as Christian life: whoever observed festivals in this way, prayed in this way, fasted in this way, and dressed in this way was said to live a spiritual and Christian life. On the other hand, other necessary good works were considered secular and unspiritual: the works which everybody is obliged to do according to his calling—for example, that a husband should labor to support his wife and children and bring them up in the fear of God, that a wife should bear children and care for them, that a prince and magistrates should govern land and people, etc. Such works, commanded by God, were to be regarded as secular and imperfect, while traditions were to be given the glamorous title of alone being holy and perfect works. Accordingly there was no end or limit to the making of such traditions.

necessary
good works...

In the third place, such traditions have turned out to be a grievous burden to consciences, for it was not possible to keep all the traditions, and yet the people were of the opinion that they were a necessary service of God. Gerson writes that many fell into despair on this account, and some even committed suicide, because they had not heard anything of the consolation of the grace of Christ. We can see in the writings of the summists[2] and canonists[3] how consciences have been confused, for they undertook to collate the traditions and sought mitigations to relieve consciences, but they were so occupied with such efforts that they neglected all wholesome Christian teachings about more important things, such as faith, consolation in severe trials, and the like. Many devout and learned people before our time have also complained that such traditions caused so much strife in the church that godly people were thereby hindered from coming to a right knowledge of Christ. Gerson and others have complained bitterly about this.[4] In fact, Augustine was also displeased that consciences were burdened with so many traditions, and he taught in this connection that they were not to be considered necessary observances.[5]

Our teachers have not taught concerning these matters out of malice or contempt of spiritual authority, but dire need has compelled them to give instruction about the aforementioned errors which have arisen from a wrong estimation of tradition. The Gospel demands that the teaching about faith should and must be emphasized in the church, but this teaching cannot be understood if it is supposed that grace is earned through self-chosen works.

It is therefore taught that grace cannot be earned, God cannot be reconciled, and sin cannot be atoned for by observing the said human traditions. Accordingly they should not be made into a necessary service of God. Rea-

sons for this shall be cited from the Scriptures. In Matt.
15:1-20 Christ defends the apostles for not observing the
customary traditions, and he adds, "In vain do they worship me, teaching as doctrines the precepts of men" (Matt.
15:9). Since he calls them vain service, they must not be
necessary. Thereupon Christ says, "Not what goes into
the mouth defiles a man."[6] Paul also says in Rom. 14:17,
"The kingdom of God does not mean food and drink,"
and in Col. 2:16 he says, "Let no one pass judgment on
you in questions of food and drink or with regard to a
festival," etc. In Acts 15:10, 11 Peter says, "Why do
you make trial of God by putting a yoke upon the neck of
the disciples which neither our fathers nor we have been
able to bear? But we believe that we shall be saved through
the grace of the Lord Jesus, just as they will." Here Peter
forbids the burdening of consciences with additional outward ceremonies, whether of Moses or of another. In
I Tim. 4:1, 3, such prohibitions as forbid food or marriage are called a doctrine of the devil, for it is diametrically
opposed to the Gospel to institute or practice such works
for the purpose of earning forgiveness of sin or with the
notion that nobody is a Christian unless he performs such
services.

Although our teachers are, like Jovinian,[7] accused of
forbidding mortification and discipline, their writings reveal
something quite different. They have always taught concerning the holy cross that Christians are obliged to suffer,
and this is true and real rather than invented mortification.

They also teach that everybody is under obligation to
conduct himself, with reference to such bodily exercise as
fasting and other discipline, so that he does not give occasion to sin, but not as if he earned grace by such works.
Such bodily exercise should not be limited to certain specified days but should be practiced continually. Christ
speaks of this in Luke 21:34, "Take heed to yourselves

lest your hearts be weighed down with dissipation," and again, "This kind of demon cannot be driven out by anything but fasting and prayer."[8] Paul said that he pommeled his body and subdued it,[9] and by this he indicated that it is not the purpose of mortification to merit grace but to keep the body in such a condition that one can perform the duties required by one's calling. Thus fasting in itself is not rejected, but what is rejected is making a necessary service of fasts on prescribed days and with specified foods, for this confuses consciences.

prescribed days
...specified foods

We on our part also retain many ceremonies and traditions (such as the liturgy of the Mass and various canticles, festivals, and the like) which serve to preserve order in the church. At the same time, however, the people are instructed that such outward forms of service do not make us righteous before God and that they are to be observed without burdening consciences, which is to say that it is not a sin to omit them if this is done without causing scandal. The ancient Fathers maintained such liberty with respect to outward ceremonies, for in the East they kept Easter at a time different from that in Rome.[10] When some regarded this difference as divisive of the church, they were admonished by others that it was not necessary to maintain uniformity in such customs. Irenaeus said, "Disagreement in fasting does not destroy unity in faith,"[11] and there is a statement in Dist. 12 that such disagreement in human ordinances is not in conflict with the unity of Christendom.[12] Moreover, the Tripartite History, Book 9, gathers many examples of dissimilar church usages

and adds the profitable Christian observation, "It was not
the intention of the apostles to institute holy days but to
teach faith and love."[13]

XXVII. Monastic Vows

In discussing monastic vows it is necessary to begin by
considering what opinions have hitherto been held concerning them, what kind of life was lived in the monasteries, and how many of the daily observances in them
were contrary not only to the Word of God but also to
papal canons. In the days of St. Augustine monastic
life was voluntary. Later, when true discipline and doctrine had become corrupted, monastic vows were invented,
and the attempt was made to restore discipline by means
of these vows as if in a well-conceived prison.[1]

In addition to monastic vows many other requirements
were imposed, and such fetters and burdens were laid on
many before they had attained an appropriate age.[2]

Many persons also entered monastic life ignorantly,
for although they were not too young, they had not sufficiently appreciated or understood their strength. All of
those who were thus ensnared and entangled were pressed
and compelled to remain, in spite of the fact that even the
papal canons might have set many of them free.[3] The
practice was stricter in women's convents than in those
of men, though it would have been seemly to show more
consideration to women as the weaker sex. Such severity
and rigor displeased many devout people in the past, for
they must have seen that both boys and girls were thrust
into monasteries to provide for their maintenance. They
must also have seen what evils came from this arrangement, what scandals and burdened consciences resulted.
Many people complained that in such a momentous matter the canons were not strictly adhered to. Besides,
monastic vows gained such a reputation, as is well known,

that many monks with even a little understanding were displeased.

It was claimed that monastic vows were equal to Baptism, and that by monastic life one could earn forgiveness of sin and justification before God.[4] What is more, they added that monastic life not only earned righteousness and godliness, but also that by means of this life both the precepts and the counsels included in the Gospel were kept,[5] and so monastic vows were praised more highly than Baptism. They also claimed that more merit could be obtained by monastic life than by all other states of life instituted by God—whether the office of pastor and preacher, or ruler, prince, lord, or the like, all of whom serve in their appointed calling according to God's Word and command without invented spirituality. None of these things can be denied, for they are found in their own books.

Furthermore, those who were thus ensnared and inveigled into a monastery learned little about Christ. Formerly the monasteries had conducted schools of Holy Scripture and other branches of learning which are profitable to the Christian church, so that pastors and bishops were taken from monasteries. But now the picture is changed. In former times people gathered and adopted monastic life for the purpose of learning the Scriptures, but now it is claimed that monastic life is of such a nature that thereby God's grace and righteousness before God are earned. In fact, it is called a state of perfection[6] and

it is called
a state of
perfection

is regarded as far superior to the other estates instituted by God. All this is mentioned, without misrepresentation, in order that one may better grasp and understand what our teachers teach and preach.

For one thing, it is taught among us with regard to those who desire to marry that all those who are not suited for celibacy have the power, right, and authority to marry, for vows cannot nullify God's order and command. God's command in I Cor. 7:2 reads, "Because of the temptation to immorality, each man should have his own wife and each woman her own husband." It is not alone God's command that urges, drives, and compels us to do this, but God's creation and order also direct all to marriage who are not endowed with the gift of virginity by a special act of God. This appears from God's own words in Gen. 2:18, "It is not good that the man should be alone; I will make him a helper fit for him."

What objection may be raised to this? No matter how much one extols the vow and the obligation, no matter how highly one exalts them, it is still impossible to abrogate God's command. Learned men say that a vow made contrary to papal canons is not binding.[7] How much less must be their obligation, lawfulness, and power when they are contrary to God's command!

If there were no reasons which allowed annulment of the obligation of a vow, the popes could not have dispensed and released men from such obligation, for no man has the right to cancel an obligation which is derived from divine law. Consequently the popes were well aware that some amelioration ought to be exercised in connection with this obligation and have often given dispensations, as in the case of the king of Aragon[8] and many others. If dispensations were granted for the maintenance of temporal interests, how much more should dispensations be granted for necessities of men's souls!

Why, then, do our opponents insist so strongly that vows must be kept without first ascertaining whether a vow is of the proper sort? For a vow must involve what is possible and voluntary and must be uncoerced.[9] Yet it is commonly known to what an extent perpetual chastity lies within human power and ability, and there are few, whether men or women, who have taken monastic vows of themselves, willingly, and after due consideration. Before they came to a right understanding they were persuaded to take monastic vows, and sometimes they have been compelled and forced to do so. Accordingly it is not right to argue so rashly and insistently about the obligation of vows inasmuch as it is generally conceded that it belongs to the very nature and character of a vow that it should be voluntary and should be assumed only after due consideration and counsel.

Several canons and papal regulations annul vows that are made under the age of fifteen years.[10] They hold that before this age one does not possess sufficient understanding to determine or arrange the order of one's whole future life. Another canon concedes still more years to human frailty, for it prohibits the taking of monastic vows before the eighteenth year.[11] On the basis of this provision most monastics have excuse and reason for leaving their monasteries inasmuch as a majority of them entered the cloister in their childhood, before attaining such age.

Finally, although the breaking of monastic vows might be censured, it would not follow that the marriage of those who broke them should be dissolved. For St. Augustine says in his *Nuptiarum,* Question 27, Chapter I, that such a marriage should not be dissolved,[12] and St. Augustine is no inconsiderable authority in the Christian church, even though some have subsequently differed from him.

Although God's command concerning marriage frees

and releases many from monastic vows, our teachers
offer still more reasons why monastic vows are null and
void. For all service of God that is chosen and instituted
by men to obtain righteousness and God's grace without
the command and authority of God is opposed to God
and the holy Gospel and contrary to God's command.
So Christ himself says in Matt. 15:9, "In vain do they
worship me, teaching as doctrines the precepts of men."
St. Paul also teaches everywhere that one is not to seek
for righteousness in the precepts and services invented
by men but that righteousness and godliness in God's
sight come from faith and trust when we believe that
God receives us into his favor for the sake of Christ,
his only Son.

It is quite evident that the monks have taught and
preached that their invented spiritual life makes satisfaction for sin and obtains God's grace and righteousness.[13]
What is this but to diminish the glory and honor of the
grace of Christ and deny the righteousness of faith? It
follows from this that the customary vows were an im-
proper and false service of God. Therefore they are not
binding, for an ungodly vow, made contrary to God's
command, is null and void. Even the canons teach that
an oath should not be an obligation to sin.[14]

St. Paul says in Gal. 5:4, "You are severed from Christ,
you who would be justified by the law; you have fallen
away from grace." In the same way, those who would
be justified by vows are severed from Christ and have
fallen away from God's grace, for they rob Christ, who
alone justifies, of his honor and bestow this honor on
their vows and monastic life.

One cannot deny that the monks have taught and
preached that they were justified and earned forgiveness
of sins by their vows and their monastic life and observances. In fact, they have invented a still more indecent

and absurd claim, namely, that they could apply their good works to others. If one were inclined to count up all these claims for the purpose of casting them into their teeth, how many items could be assembled which the monks themselves are now ashamed of and wish had never occurred! Besides all this, they persuaded the people that the invented spiritual estate of the orders was Christian perfection.[15] Certainly this is exaltation of works as a means of attaining justification. Now, it is no small offense in the Christian church that the people should be presented with such a service of God, invented by men without the command of God, and should be taught that such a service would make men good and righteous before God. For righteousness of faith, which should be emphasized above all else in the Christian church, is obscured when man's eyes are dazzled with this curious angelic spirituality and sham of poverty, humility, and chastity.

Besides, the commands of God and true and proper service of God are obscured when people are told that monks alone are in a state of perfection. For this is Christian perfection: that we fear God honestly with our whole hearts, and yet have sincere confidence, faith, and trust that for Christ's sake we have a gracious, merciful God; that we may and should ask and pray God for those things of which we have need, and confidently expect help from him in every affliction connected with our particular calling and station in life; and that meanwhile we do good works for others and diligently attend to our calling. True perfection and right service of God consist of these things and not of mendicancy or wearing a black or gray cowl, etc. However, the common people, hearing the state of celibacy praised above all measure, draw many harmful conclusions from such false exaltation of monastic life, for it follows that their consciences are troubled because they are married. When the common man hears that only mendicants are perfect, he is uncertain whether he can keep his possessions and engage in business without sin. When the people hear that it is only a counsel[16] not to take revenge, it is natural that some should conclude that it is not sinful to take revenge outside of the exercise of their office. Still others think that it is not right at all for Christians, even in the government, to avenge wrong.

seeking a life
more pleasing
to God...

Many instances are also recorded of men who forsook wife and child, and also their civil office, to take shelter in a monastery. This, they said, is fleeing from the world and seeking a life more pleasing to God than the other. They were unable to understand that one is to serve God by observing the commands God has given and not by keeping the commands invented by men. That is a good and perfect state of life which has God's command to support it; on the other hand, that is a dangerous state of life which does not have God's command behind it. About such matters it was necessary to give the people proper instruction.

In former times Gerson censured the error of the monks concerning perfection and indicated that it was an innovation of his time to speak of monastic life as a state of perfection.[17]

Thus there are many godless opinions and errors associated with monastic vows: that they justify and render men righteous before God, that they constitute Christian perfection, that they are the means of fulfilling both evangelical counsels and precepts, and that they furnish the works of supererogation[18] which we are not obligated to render to God. Inasmuch as all these things are false, useless, and invented, monastic vows are null and void.

XXVIII. The Power of Bishops

Many and various things have been written in former times about the power of bishops, and some have improperly confused the power of bishops with the temporal sword. Out of this careless confusion many serious wars, tumults, and uprisings have resulted because the bishops, under pretext of the power given them by Christ, have not only introduced new forms of worship and burdened consciences with reserved cases[1] and violent use of the ban, but have also presumed to set up and depose kings and emperors according to their pleasure. Such outrage has long since been condemned by learned and devout people in Christendom. On this account our teachers have been compelled, for the sake of comforting consciences, to point out the difference between spiritual and temporal power, sword, and authority, and they have taught that because of God's command both authorities and powers are to be honored and esteemed with all reverence as the two highest gifts of God on earth.

Our teachers assert that according to the Gospel the power of keys or the power of bishops is a power and command of God to preach the Gospel, to forgive and retain sins, and to administer and distribute the sacraments. For Christ sent out the apostles with this command, "As the Father has sent me, even so I send you. Receive the Holy Spirit. If you forgive the sins of any, they are forgiven; if you retain the sins of any, they are retained" (John 20:21–23).

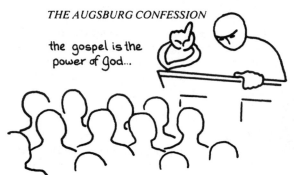

the gospel is the power of God...

This power of keys or of bishops is used and exercised only by teaching and preaching the Word of God and by administering the sacraments (to many persons or to individuals, depending on one's calling). In this way are imparted not bodily but eternal things and gifts, namely, eternal righteousness, the Holy Spirit, and eternal life. These gifts cannot be obtained except through the office of preaching and of administering the holy sacraments, for St. Paul says, "The gospel is the power of God for salvation to everyone who has faith."[2] Inasmuch as the power of the church or of bishops bestows eternal gifts and is used and exercised only through the office of preaching, it does not interfere at all with government or temporal authority. Temporal authority is concerned with matters altogether different from the Gospel. Temporal power does not protect the soul, but with the sword and physical penalties it protects body and goods from the power of others.

Therefore, the two authorities, the spiritual and the temporal, are not to be mingled or confused, for the spiritual power has its commission to preach the Gospel and administer the sacraments. Hence it should not invade the function of the other, should not set up and depose kings, should not annul temporal laws or undermine obedience to government, should not make or prescribe to the temporal power laws concerning worldly matters. Christ himself said, "My kingship is not of this world,"[3] and again, "Who made me a judge or divider over you?"[4] Paul also wrote in Phil. 3:20, "Our commonwealth is in heaven," and in II Cor. 10:4, 5, "The weapons of our warfare are not worldly but have divine power to destroy strongholds and every proud obstacle to the knowledge of God."

Thus our teachers distinguish the two authorities and the functions of the two powers, directing that both be held in honor as the highest gifts of God on earth.

In cases where bishops possess temporal authority and the sword, they possess it not as bishops by divine right, but by human, imperial right, bestowed by Roman emperors and kings for the temporal administration of their lands. Such authority has nothing at all to do with the office of the Gospel.

According to divine right, therefore, it is the office of the bishop to preach the Gospel, forgive sins, judge doctrine and condemn doctrine that is contrary to the Gospel, and exclude from the Christian community the ungodly whose wicked conduct is manifest. All this is to be done not by human power but by God's Word alone. On this account parish ministers and churches are bound to be obedient to the bishops according to the saying of Christ in Luke 10:16, "He who hears you hears me." On the other hand, if they teach, introduce, or institute anything contrary to the Gospel, we have God's command not to be obedient in such cases, for Christ says in Matt. 7:15, "Beware of false prophets." St. Paul also writes in Gal. 1:8, "Even if we, or an angel from heaven, should preach to you a gospel contrary to that which we preached to you, let him be accursed," and in II Cor. 13:8, "We cannot do anything against the truth, but only for the truth." Again Paul refers to "the authority which the Lord has given me for building up and not for tearing down."[5] Canon law requires the same in Part II, Question 7, in the chapters "Sacerdotes" and "Oves."[6]

St. Augustine also writes in his reply to the letters of Petilian that one should not obey even regularly elected bishops if they err or if they teach or command something contrary to the divine Holy Scriptures.[7]

Whatever other power and jurisdiction bishops may have in various matters (for example, in matrimonial cases and in tithes),[8] they have these by virtue of human right. However, when bishops are negligent in the performance of such duties, the princes are obliged, whether they like to or not, to administer justice to their subjects for the sake of peace and to prevent discord and great disorder in their lands.

Besides, there is dispute as to whether bishops have the power to introduce ceremonies in the church or establish regulations concerning foods, holy days, and the different orders of the clergy. Those who attribute such power to bishops cite Christ's saying in John 16:12, 13, "I have yet many things to say to you, but you cannot bear them now. When the Spirit of truth comes, he will guide you into all the truth."[9] They also cite the example in Acts 15:20, 29, where the eating of blood and what is strangled was forbidden. Besides, they appeal to the fact that the Sabbath was changed to Sunday—contrary, as they say, to the Ten Commandments. No case is appealed to and urged so insistently as the change of the Sabbath, for thereby they wish to maintain that the power of the church is indeed great because the church has dispensed from and altered part of the Ten Commandments.[10]

Concerning this question our teachers assert that bishops do not have power to institute or establish anything contrary to the Gospel, as has been indicated above and as is taught by canon law throughout the whole of the ninth Distinction.[11] It is patently contrary to God's command and Word to make laws out of opinions or to require that they be observed in order to make satisfaction for sins and obtain grace, for the glory of Christ's merit is blasphemed when we presume to earn grace by such ordinances. It is also apparent that because of this notion human ordinances have multiplied beyond calculation while the teaching concerning faith and righteousness of faith has almost been suppressed. Almost every day new holy days and new fasts have been prescribed, new ceremonies and new venerations of saints have been instituted in order that by such works grace and everything good might be earned from God.

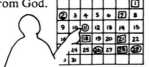

new holy
days...
new fasts

Again, those who institute human ordinances also act contrary to God's command when they attach sin to foods, days, and similar things and burden Christendom with the bondage of the law, as if in order to earn God's grace there had to be a service of God among Christians like the Levitical[12] service, and as if God had commanded the apostles and bishops to institute it, as some have written. It is quite believable that some bishops were misled by the example of the law of Moses. The result was that countless regulations came into being—for example, that it is a mortal sin to do manual work on holy days (even when it does not give offense to others), that it is a mortal sin to omit the seven hours,[13] that some foods defile the conscience, that fasting is a work by which God is reconciled, that in a reserved case sin is not forgiven unless forgiveness is secured from the person for whom the case is reserved, in spite of the fact that canon law says nothing of the reservation of guilt but speaks only about the reservation of ecclesiastical penalties.[14]

Where did the bishops get the right and power to impose such requirements on Christendom to ensnare men's consciences? In Acts 15:10 St. Peter forbids putting a yoke on the neck of the disciples. And St. Paul said in II Cor. 10:8 that authority was given for building up and not for tearing down. Why, then, do they multiply sins with such requirements?

Yet there are clear passages of divine Scripture which forbid the establishment of such regulations for the purpose of earning God's grace or as if they were necessary for salvation. Thus St. Paul says in Col. 2:16, "Let no one pass judgment on you in questions of food and drink or with regard to a festival or a new moon or a sabbath. These are only a shadow of what is to come; but the substance belongs to Christ." Again in Col. 2:20–23, "If with Christ you died to the regulations of the world, why do you live as if you still belonged to the world? Why do you submit to regulations, 'Do not handle, Do not taste, Do not touch' (referring to things which all perish as they are used), according to human precepts and doctrines? These have an appearance of wisdom." In Tit. 1:14 St. Paul also forbids giving heed to Jewish myths or to commands of men who reject the truth.

Christ himself says concerning those who urge human ordinances on people, "Let them alone; they are blind guides" (Matt. 15:14). He rejects such service of God and says, "Every plant which my heavenly Father has not planted will be rooted up" (Matt. 15:13).

If, then, bishops have the power to burden the churches with countless requirements and thus ensnare consciences, why does the divine Scripture so frequently forbid the making and keeping of human regulations? Why does it call them doctrines of the devil?[15] Is it possible that the Holy Spirit warned against them for nothing?

Inasmuch as such regulations as have been instituted as necessary to propitiate God and merit grace are contrary to the Gospel, it is not at all proper for the bishops to require such services of God. It is necessary to preserve the teaching of Christian liberty in Christendom, namely, that bondage to the law is not necessary for justification, as St. Paul writes in Gal. 5:1, "For freedom Christ has set us free; stand fast, therefore, and do not submit again to a yoke of slavery." For the chief article of the Gospel must be maintained, namely, that we obtain the grace of God through faith in Christ without our merits; we do not merit it by services of God instituted by men.

What are we to say, then, about Sunday and other similar church ordinances and ceremonies? To this our teachers reply[16] that bishops or pastors may make regulations so that everything in the churches is done in good order, but not as a means of obtaining God's grace or making satisfaction for sins, nor in order to bind men's consciences by considering these things necessary services of God and counting it a sin to omit their observance even when this is done without offense. So St. Paul directed in I Cor. 11:5 that women should cover their heads in the assembly. He also directed that in the assembly preachers should not all speak at once, but one after another, in order.[17]

It is proper for the Christian assembly to keep such ordinances for the sake of love and peace, to be obedient to the bishops and parish ministers in such matters, and to observe the regulations in such a way that one does not give offense to another and so that there may be no disorder or unbecoming conduct in the church. However, consciences should not be burdened by contending that such things are necessary for salvation or that it is a sin to omit them, even when no offense is given to others, just as no one would say that a woman commits a sin if without offense to others she goes out with uncovered head.

consciences should not be burdened

Of like character is the observance of Sunday, Easter, Pentecost, and similar holy days and usages. Those who consider the appointment of Sunday in place of the Sabbath as a necessary institution are very much mistaken, for the Holy Scriptures have abrogated the Sabbath and teach that after the revelation of the Gospel all ceremonies of the old law may be omitted. Nevertheless, because it was necessary to appoint a certain day so that the people might know when they ought to assemble, the Christian church appointed Sunday for this purpose, and it was the more inclined and pleased to do this in order that the people might have an example of Christian liberty and might know that the keeping neither of the Sabbath nor of any other day is necessary.

There are many faulty discussions[18] of the transformation of the law, of the ceremonies of the New Testament, and of the change of the Sabbath, all of which have arisen from the false and erroneous opinion that in Christendom one must have services of God like the Levitical or Jewish services and that Christ commanded the apostles and bishops to devise new ceremonies which would be necessary for salvation. Such errors were introduced into Christendom when the righteousness of faith was no longer taught and preached with clarity and purity. Some argue that although Sunday must not be kept as of divine obligation, it must nevertheless be kept as almost of divine obligation, and they prescribe the kind and amount of work that may be done on the day of rest. What are such discussions but snares of conscience? For although they undertake to lighten and mitigate human regulations,[19] yet there can be no moderation or mitigation as long as the opinion remains and prevails that their observance is necessary. And this opinion will remain as long as there is no understanding of the righteousness of faith and Christian liberty.

The apostles directed that one should abstain from blood and from what is strangled. Who observes this prohibition now? Those who do not observe it commit no sin, for the apostles did not wish to burden consciences with such bondage but forbade such eating for a time to avoid offense. One must pay attention to the chief article of Christian doctrine, and this is not abrogated by the decree.[20]

Scarcely any of the ancient canons are observed according to the letter, and many of the regulations fall into disuse from day to day even among those who observe such ordinances most jealously. It is impossible to give counsel or help to consciences unless this mitigation is practiced, that one recognizes that such rules are not to be deemed necessary and that disregard of them does not injure consciences.

The bishops might easily retain the obedience of men if they did not insist on the observance of regulations which cannot be kept without sin. Now, however, they administer the sacrament in one kind and prohibit administration in both kinds. Again, they forbid clergymen to marry and admit no one to the ministry unless he first swears an oath that he will not preach this doctrine, although there is no doubt that it is in accord with the holy Gospel. Our churches do not ask that the bishops should restore peace and unity at the expense of their honor and dignity (though it is incumbent on the bishops to do this, too, in case of need), but they ask only that the bishops relax certain unreasonable burdens which did not exist in the church in former times and which were introduced contrary to the custom of the universal Christian church. Perhaps there was some reason for introducing them, but they are not adapted to our times. Nor can it be denied that some regulations were adopted from want of understanding. Accordingly the bishops ought to be so gracious as to temper these regulations inasmuch as such changes do not destroy the unity of Christian churches. For many regulations devised by men have with the passing of time fallen into disuse and are not obligatory, as papal law itself testifies.[21] If, however, this is impossible and they cannot be persuaded to mitigate or abrogate human regulations which are not to be observed without sin, we are bound to follow the apostolic rule which commands us to obey God rather than men.[22]

St. Peter forbids the bishops to exercise lordship as if they had power to coerce the churches according to their will.[23] It is not our intention to find ways of reducing the bishops' power, but we desire and pray that they may not coerce our consciences to sin. If they are unwilling to do this and ignore our petition, let them consider how they will answer for it in God's sight, inasmuch as by their obstinacy they offer occasion for division and schism, which they should in truth help to prevent.

[CONCLUSION]

These are the chief articles that are regarded as controversial. Although we could have mentioned many more abuses and wrongs, to avoid prolixity and undue length we have indicated only the principal ones. The others can readily be weighed in the light of these. In the past there have been grave complaints about indulgences, pilgrimages, and misuse of the ban. Parish ministers also had endless quarrels with monks about the hearing of confessions, about burials, about sermons on special occasions, and about countless other matters. All these things we have discreetly passed over for the common good in order that the chief points at issue may better be perceived.

It must not be thought that anything has been said or introduced out of hatred or for the purpose of injuring anybody, but we have related only matters which we have considered it necessary to adduce and mention in order that it may be made very clear that we have introduced nothing, either in doctrine or in ceremonies, that is contrary to Holy Scripture or the universal Christian church. For it is manifest and evident (to speak without boasting) that we have diligently and with God's help prevented any new and godless teaching from creeping into our churches and gaining the upper hand in them.

In keeping with the summons,[1] we have desired to present the above articles as a declaration of our confession and the teaching of our preachers. If anyone should consider that it is lacking in some respect, we are ready to present further information on the basis of the divine Holy Scripture.

Your Imperial Majesty's most obedient servants:

> JOHN, duke of Saxony, elector
> GEORGE, margrave of Brandenburg
> ERNEST, duke of Lüneburg
> PHILIP, landgrave of Hesse
> JOHN FREDERICK, duke of Saxony
> FRANCIS, duke of Lüneburg
> WOLFGANG, prince of Anhalt
> Mayor and council of Nuremberg
> Mayor and council of Reutlingen

NOTES

1 Latin: in the writings of either party.

2 The actual language of the imperial summons is here reproduced.

3 The diets, or parliamentary assemblies of the empire, were made up of the seven princes who were called "electors," of the other princes, and of the representatives of the free cities.

4 Elector John of Saxony and Landgrave Philip of Hesse arrived in Augsburg ahead of the emperor.

5 At the formal opening of the diet on June 20, 1530.

6 At the last minute the presentation was postponed from Friday (June 24) to Saturday (June 25).

7 Latin adds: not only once, but many times.

8 The diet of 1527 in Ratisbon was poorly attended and adjourned without accomplishing much.

9 The peace of Barcelona (1529) was followed by an alliance (1529) and the coronation of the emperor in February, 1530.

10 Latin: If the outcome should be such that these differences between us and the other party should not be amicably settled.

ARTICLE I

1 The titles of some articles, here enclosed in brackets, were inserted in and after 1533.

2 The Nicene Creed.

3 The terms *hypostasis* in Greek or *persona* in Latin were used in the ancient church to repudiate Modalism, which regarded the Father, Son, and Holy Spirit as three modes or manifestations of the one God.

4 A religion based on Persian dualism combined with Christian and other elements, founded in the third century by Mani and named after him. The Albigensians of the late Middle Ages held similar notions.

5 Gnostics of the second century who took their name from Valentinus.

6 Followers of Arius who were condemned at the Council of Nicaea in 325 and who held that the Son was created and was of different "substance" from the Father.

7 Followers of Eunomius, an extreme Arian of the late fourth century.

8 The Reformers frequently referred to Mohammedanism as an anti-Trinitarian heresy.

9 Followers of Paul of Samosata, who taught in the third century that Jesus was a man specially endowed by the Spirit. The "new Samosatenes" were anti-Trinitarian spiritualists of the sixteenth century like John Campanus and Hans Denck.

ARTICLE II

1 The traditional term *Erbsünde* is employed.

2 Followers of Pelagius, who at the beginning of the fifth century taught that man is not sinful by nature and can be saved by an act of his own will aided by God's grace. The Reformers charged Ulrich Zwingli and the scholastic theologians with teaching Pelagianism.

ARTICLE V

1 This title would be misleading if it were not observed (as the text of the article makes clear) that the Reformers thought of "the office of the ministry" in other than clerical terms.

2 For example, Sebastian Franck and Caspar Schwenkfeld taught in the sixteenth century that the Spirit comes to men without means.

ARTICLE VI

1 In contrast to unnecessary works which are not commanded by God, mentioned below in Art. XX and XXVI.

2 Ambrosiaster, *The First Epistle to the Corinthians,* 1:4.

ARTICLE VIII

1 Rigorists of the fourth century who denied the validity of the ministry of those who apostatized under persecution.

ARTICLE XI

1 Required by the Fourth Lateran Council (1215), cap. 21.

ARTICLE XII

1 The Latin text sharpens the distinction from the Roman sacrament of penance (contrition, confession, absolution, and satisfaction).

2 Such was the teaching, for example, of Hans Denck.

3 Rigorists in Rome during the third century who denied restoration, even after repentance, to those who were guilty of grave sins.

ARTICLE XV

1 Among Lutherans at this time numerous saints' days were abolished and most of the apostles' days were transferred to the succeeding Sundays, but many of the festivals of the church year were retained.

2 Such fast days of the Roman Church as Fridays, ember days, days in Lent, etc.

ARTICLE XVI

1 The Anabaptists actually differed from one another in their attitudes toward the state, marriage, and economic life, but some took the negative position here indicated.

2 The notion of Christian perfection here referred to was embodied in monasticism (called the "state of perfection") and was embraced by some Anabaptists. See also Art. XXVII, below.

3 *Wahrhaftige Gottesordnung.*

ARTICLE XVII

1 Taught, for example, by Hans Denck and Melchior Rinck.

2 Incited by Hans Hut and some Jews in Worms, Melchior Rinck predicted that the millennium would be ushered in during Easter, 1530.

ARTICLE XVIII

1 *Hypomnesticon contra Pelagianos et Coelestinianos,* III, 4, 5, ascribed to Augustine in older collections of his works.

2 Early varients add at this point: Rejected here are those who teach that we can keep the commandments of God without grace and the Holy Spirit. For although we are by nature capable of performing the outward act enjoined in a commandment, we are not capable of performing in our hearts what the commandments supremely require, namely, truly to fear, love, and trust God, etc.

ARTICLE XX

1 Societies of laymen for devotional exercises and good works.

2 *The Spirit and the Letter,* XIX, 34.

3 Cf. James 2:19.

4 *Homilies on the Epistle of John to the Parthians,* X, 2.

ARTICLE XXI

1 Fathers of the ancient church in the West.

ARTICLE XXII

1 In the West the cup was generally given to the laity until the thirteenth century.

2 Cyprian, Epistle 57.

3 Jerome, *Commentary on Zephaniah,* 3.

4 Gratian, *Decretum,* Part III, *De consecratione,* dist. 2, chap. 12.

5 Nicholas of Cusa (1401–1464), Epistle III to the Bohemians, refers the authorization for the withdrawal of the cup to the Fourth Lateran Council, 1215.

6 Reference is to the observance of the Corpus Christi festival on the Thursday following Trinity Sunday. The Evangelical princes refused to participate in the Corpus Christi procession in Augsburg on June 16, 1530. Even "carrying the sacrament across the street" was later forbidden.

ARTICLE XXIII

1 Although the requirement of celibacy was frequently asserted and practiced in earlier centuries, it was not until the end of the eleventh century that it was generally enforced by Pope Gregory VII. At that time most of the priests in Germany were still married.

2 Siegfried of Mayence at synods in Erfurt and Mayence in 1075.

3 Gratian, *Decretum,* Part I, dist. 82, chap. 2–5; also dist. 84, chap. 4. The Council of Nicaea refused to require celibacy; see Evagrius, *Ecclesiastical History,* I, 11.

4 In his history of the popes (1479) the Italian humanist Bartolomeo Platina reported Pope Pius II (1458–1464) as saying this.

5 Gratian, *Decretum,* Part I, dist. 34, chap. 7; Part II, chap. 1, q.7, c.5.

6 Cyprian, *Epistles,* 62, 2. The text refers to the numbering of Cyprian's letters adopted by Erasmus.

7 Gratian, *Decretum,* Part II, Chap. 20, q.1, c.5, 7, 9, 10, 14, 15.

ARTICLE XXIV

1 E.g., by John Eck, *404 Theses,* Nos. 269–278. This article makes it clear, of course, that retention of the Mass does not mean retention of abuses.

2 By men like Nicholas of Cusa, John Tauler, John Gerson, and Gabriel Biel.

3 I Cor. 11:27.

4 Masses said for the special intentions of individuals, often called Votive Masses.

5 Heb. 9:28; 10:10, 14.

6 Chrysostom, Homily 3 in *Epistle to the Ephesians,* chap. 1.

7 Canon 18 of the Council of Nicaea.

8 The *Tripartite Ecclesiastical History* by the Roman monk Cassiodorus (480–570) was the principal book of church history used in the late Middle Ages, and it quotes here from Socrates, *Ecclesiastical History,* V, 22.

ARTICLE XXV

1 Ps. 19:12.

2 Jer. 17:9.

3 Ps. 37:5 (Vulgate rendering).

4 Gratian, *Decretum,* Part II, chap. 33, q.3, *De poenitentia,* dist. I, c.87:4. The quotation is from Chrysostom, Homily 31, in *Epistle to the Hebrews.*

5 Gloss to Gratian, *Decretum, De poenitentia,* 5:1.

ARTICLE XXVI

1 E.g., Thomas Aquinas, *Summa theologica,* II, 2. q.147, a, 1, c.

2 Authors of such collections of cases of conscience in the Middle

Ages as Sylvester Prierias' *Summa summarum.*

3   Experts in canon law.

4   John Gerson, *The Spiritual Life,* lectio 2.

5   Augustine, Epistle 54 to Januarius, 2:2.

6   Matt. 15:11.

7   The Reformers were here misled by Jerome's slanderous misrepresentation of Jovinian, Roman ascetic of the fourth century who contended against the monastic teaching about merits and the stages of ethical perfection but not against "mortification and discipline."

8   Mark 9:29.

9   I Cor. 9:27.

10   In Asia Minor Easter was observed on the Jewish Passover while in the West, as in Palestine and Egypt, it was observed on the Sunday following.

11   In Eusebius, *Ecclesiastical History,* V. 24, 13.

12   Gratian, *Decretum,* Part I, dist. 12, chap. 10.

13   Cassiodorus, *Tripartite Ecclesiastical History,* IX, 38, quoting from Socrates, *Ecclesiastical History,* V. 22.

ARTICLE XXVII

1   Until the Benedictine Rule gained ascendency in the West, about the eighth century, there was a variety of monastic rules. Withdrawal from monastic life was originally allowable.

2   The dedication of children to monastic life by their parents was common in the Middle Ages and allowed by canon law.

3   See above, Art. XXIII.

4   The comparison of monastic profession and Baptism was common in the Middle Ages. E.g., Thomas Aquinas, *Summa theologica,* II, 2, q.189, a.3 ad 3.

5   Medieval theologians, following a development which can be traced back to Tertullian, distinguished between "precepts of the Gospel," which must be observed for salvation, and "counsels of the Gospel," which are not obligatory, but enable one to attain salvation "better and more quickly." See, e.g., Bonaventure, *Breviloquium,* V, 9; Thomas Aquinas, *Summa theologica,* II, 1, q.108, a.4.

6   E.g., Thomas Aquinas, *Summa theologica,* II, 2, q.186, a, 1, c.

7   Gratian, *Decretum,* Part II, chap. 20, q.4, c.2, states that a vow made by a monk without the consent of his abbot is without effect.

8   Ramiro, II, a monk, was released from his vows after the death of his childless brother so that he might assume the throne.

9   Cf. Thomas Aquinas, *Summa theologica,* II, 2, q.88, a.1, 8.

10   Gratian, *Decretum,* Part II, chap. 20, q.1, c.10.

11   *Ibid.,* chap. 5.

12   Augustine, *De bono viduitatis,* chap. 9.

13   Cf. Thomas Aquinas, as cited above under Art. XXVII (note 4).

14   Gratian, *Decretum,* II, chap. 22, q.4, c.22.

15   See above, Art. XXVII.

16 A so-called "evangelical counsel." See above, Art. XXVII, and note (5).

17 Among many other places, see John Gerson, *Evangelical Counsels,* in *Opera,* II, 680.

18 Works in addition to those which every Christian is obligated to perform. See above, Art. XXVII.

ARTICLE XXVIII

1   Cases in which absolution was reserved for bishops or the pope.
2   Rom. 1:16.
3   John 18:36.
4   Luke 12:14.
5   II Cor. 13:10.
6   Gratian, *Decretum,* Part II, q.7, c.8, 13.
7   Augustine, *The Unity of the Church,* 11, 28.
8   The payment to the church of one-tenth of the gross income from all lands and industries was required since the early Middle Ages.
9   This passage was cited by John Eck in his *Handbook of Commonplaces against Luther and Other Enemies of the Church* (1525), Nos. 1, 15.
10 Cf. Thomas Aquinas, *Summa theologica,* II, q.122, a.4 ad 4.
11 Gratian, *Decretum,* Part I, dist. 9, c.8ff.
12 I.e., Jewish.
13 The canonical hours, or the seven daily hours of prayer, prescribed for monastics and others.
14 See note (1) under Art. XXVIII.
15 Cf. I Tim. 4:1.
16 A reply was called for since John Eck had just attacked the Evangelicals for erroneous views of the Lord's Day. See Eck, *404 Theses,* Nos. 177–179.
17 I Cor. 14:30.
18 E.g., Thomas Aquinas, *Summa theologica,* II, 1, q.103.
19 Cf. above, Art. XXVI.
20 The so-called apostolic decree in Acts 15:23–29.
21 E.g., the penitential canons of the ancient church were supplanted in the early Middle Ages when the sacrament of penance developed.
22 Acts 5:29.
23 I Pet. 5:2.

CONCLUSION

1   See above, Preface.